## DATE DUE

| FEB 21 2013 | |
| APR - 9 2013 | |
| | |
| | |
| | |
| | |
| | |
| | |
| | |
| | |
| | |
| | |
| | |
| | |
| | |
| | |
| | |
| | |
| | |
| | |

PRINTED IN U.S.A.

# BEASTS

By S.L. Hamilton

# VISIT US AT
# WWW.ABDOPUBLISHING.COM

Published by ABDO Publishing Company, 8000 West 78th Street, Suite 310, Edina, MN 55439. Copyright ©2011 by Abdo Consulting Group, Inc. International copyrights reserved in all countries. No part of this book may be reproduced in any form without written permission from the publisher. A&D Xtreme™ is a trademark and logo of ABDO Publishing Company.

Printed in the United States of America, North Mankato, Minnesota.
052010
092010

 PRINTED ON RECYCLED PAPER

Editor: John Hamilton
Graphic Design: Sue Hamilton
Cover Design:  John Hamilton
Cover Photo:  Photo Researchers
Interior Photos: Alamy-pgs 2, 3, 4, 5, 26 & 27; AP-pg 20; Arthur Rackham-pgs 14 & 15; Corbis-pgs 1, 10, 11, 16 & 17; Dave Rubert-pg 9; Fame Pictures-pgs 6 & 7; First Look International-pg 28; iStockphoto-pgs 8, 9, 22 & 23; Mary Evans Picture Library-pg 10; Metro-Goldwyn-Mayer-pg 29; Peter Arnold-pgs 6 & 15; Photo Researchers-pgs 20, 21, 24, 25, 30 & 31; Robert Kenneth Wilson-pg 21; RobRoy Menzies-pgs 12, 13 & 32; 20th Century Fox-pg 29; Walt Disney Pictures-pg 28.

Library of Congress Cataloging-in-Publication Data

Hamilton, Sue L., 1959-
  Beasts / Sue L. Hamilton.
     p. cm. --  (Xtreme monsters)
  Includes index.
  ISBN 978-1-61613-467-9
  1. Monsters--Juvenile literature.  I. Title.
  GR825.H259 2011
  398.24'54--dc22
                          2010003289

# CONTENTS

# XTREME

# BEASTS

Powerful beasts are rumored to live in the most remote areas of the land and sea. These are called cryptids. There is not enough scientific evidence to prove they exist. Are they real or imaginary?

**X̃treme Quote**

"This is where the creature goes,
Lurking in the land he knows."
~Lyrics, *The Legend of Boggy Creek*

# MAN-APE

Across the United States and Canada come tales of unusual creatures. They are described as a cross between humans and giant apes. Sometimes called Bigfoot, these beasts are  said to stand 7 to 10 feet (2-3 m) tall, walk upright, and weigh as much as 500 pounds (227 kg).

# CREATURES

**X**treme Fact

The Bigfoot Field Researchers Organization has reports of hundreds of creature sightings.

# Sasquatch

In North America's Pacific Northwest, another common name for Bigfoot is sasquatch. This is an English slurring of a word used by a Native American tribe called the Salish. In the Salish language, the word *sésquac* means "wild man."

Stompers used to create giant footprints.

Xtreme Fact True sasquatch sightings have been overshadowed by pranksters pretending to be the creature.

# Yeti

The abominable snowman, or yeti, is said to live in the Himalayan Mountains of southern Asia. Natives of the area, as well as mountain climbers, have spotted the white, gorilla-like creature, or its footprints.

Normal-size footprints become distorted and enlarged during the melting and freezing of snow in a mountainous climate.

In 1960, Edmund Hillary, the first man to climb Mount Everest, spent 10 months searching for a yeti. Hillary never found the creature, nor has it been found since.

# SEA

For centuries, sailors and people who live by the sea have told stories of the beasts that swim the dark depths of the earth's oceans.

X treme Quote

"The ocean covers 71% of the earth's surface…, yet 95% of the underwater world remains unexplored." ~National Oceanic and Atmospheric Administration

# MONSTERS

# Leviathan

The Bible tells of a giant sea creature that hissed steam from its nostrils and caused the sea to boil. Called Leviathan, the beast was said to be as big as a boat. Some believe the creature was really a blue whale, the largest animal on earth. Others believe the stories referred to an ancient sea monster of enormous size.

**Xtreme Fact**

Blue whales weigh 150 tons (136 metric tons) and can spout water 40 to 50 feet (12-15 m) in the air.

# Kraken

Norse mythology tells of a huge sea monster capable of grabbing and sinking an entire ship. The kraken, or giant squid, was said to grow up to 60 feet (18 m) in length. The deep-sea invertebrates were so big, some mistook the creatures for floating islands.

Some squids have strong, clawlike hooks on the ends of their arms.

# LIVING

A full-size Mylodon statue stands near the cave where Mylodon fossils were found in Chilean Patagonia, South America.

# FOSSILS

Could prehistoric animals still be alive in remote areas of our world? South America is believed to be home to a giant ground sloth known as a Mylodon.

treme Fact

Mylodons reportedly died out about 10,000 years ago.

Sonar equipment and underwater cameras have been used to look for "Nessie."

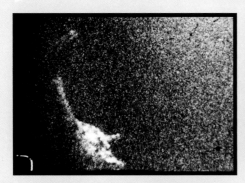

# Loch Ness Monster

Scotland's famous long-necked creature may be an ancient plesiosaur. The Loch Ness Monster is nicknamed "Nessie." Continued sightings make people wonder if an ancient sea creature still lives in the deep waters of Loch Ness.

This famous 1934 photo was a hoax. It was a clay dinosaur head on a toy sub.

# Mokele-mbembe

From Africa come reports of a monstrous animal with a long, flexible neck, an alligator-like tail, and a body about the size of an elephant. Called Mokele-mbembe, or "one that stops the flow of rivers," some believe the creature lives in the swamps of Congo, Cameroon, and Gabon.

A dinosaur statue that looks like the descriptions given of Mokele-mbembe.

**Xtreme Fact**

In 1992, a film crew captured 15 seconds of footage of what might be Mokele-mbembe in Lake Tele, Congo.

# Kongamato

Kongamato is described by African natives of western Zambia as a beaked, flying reptile. Some believe it to be a pterosaur, a creature that died out 65 million years ago. Reports of a flying demon with a wingspan of 4 to 7 feet (1 to 2 m) and a mouthful of teeth continue to make people wonder if the beast really survived the ages.

"Coming straight at me only a few feet above the water was a black thing the size of an eagle." ~Ivan Sanderson, explorer West Africa, 1932

# BLOOD

Chupacabra is a mysterious monster whose name means "goat sucker." It got its name after leaving teeth marks in the bodies of dead goats, and draining the animals of their blood. First seen on the island of Puerto Rico, it has also been reported in the southern United States, as well as Mexico, Nicaragua, and Chile.

# SUCKER

**Xtreme Quote**

"It was evil, evil looking."
~Michelle O'Donnell, after seeing
a chupacabra-like creature

# BEAST

Adventure and horror movies often feature cryptid creatures. In 2005's *Clawed: The Legend of Sasquatch*, a mysterious creature attacks a group of illegal hunters. Their deaths spark a search for the creature.

The kraken attacked ships in 2006's *Pirates of the Caribbean: Dead Man's Chest.* This Walt Disney Pictures film showed the kraken's tentacles destroying ships and people.

# MOVIES

In 2004, 20th Century Fox released *Incident at Loch Ness.* The movie's investigators interview people about monster sightings at Scotland's Loch Ness. Soon, the film crew has its own close encounter with the lake's monster.

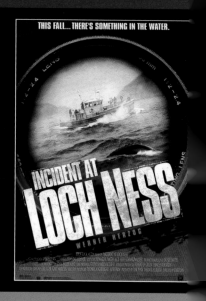

In MGM's 1989 film *Leviathan,* undersea miners come across a sunken Russian ship. Two of the miners swallow a drink that mutates them into a violent creature of the deep.

# THE

**Abominable**
Disgusting and unpleasant. The phrase "abominable snowman" may have come from a poor rendering of a Tibetan phrase for "snowfield man."

**Cryptid**
Creatures for which there is not enough scientific evidence to prove they exist, such as Bigfoot.

**Invertebrates**
Animals which do not have a backbone, such as a squid.

**Mount Everest**
The highest mountain in the world, located between Nepal and Tibet. It was first climbed in 1953 by Sir Edmund Hillary and Tenzing Norgay.

# GLOSSARY

**National Oceanic & Atmospheric Administration**
NOAA is a United States organization that researches and collects data about the world's oceans and atmosphere, and the creatures that live there.

**Pacific Northwest**
An area of North America that includes the states of Oregon and Washington, as well as part of Canada's province of British Columbia.

**Sonar**
A method of finding something submerged in water. A sonar device sends out sound waves and measures the time it takes for the echoes to return. The word comes from the phrase: sound navigation ranging.

# Index